UNCOVERING
ANCIENT ARTIFACTS

EXCAVATION
EXPLORATION

RACHAEL L. THOMAS

Checkerboard
Library

An Imprint of Abdo Publishing
abdopublishing.com

abdopublishing.com

Published by Abdo Publishing, a division of ABDO, PO Box 398166, Minneapolis, Minnesota 55439. Copyright © 2019 by Abdo Consulting Group, Inc. International copyrights reserved in all countries. No part of this book may be reproduced in any form without written permission from the publisher. Checkerboard Library™ is a trademark and logo of Abdo Publishing.

Printed in the United States of America, North Mankato, Minnesota
052018
092018

THIS BOOK CONTAINS
RECYCLED MATERIALS

Design: Sarah DeYoung, Mighty Media, Inc.
Production: Mighty Media, Inc.
Editor: Megan Borgert-Spaniol
Design elements: Mighty Media, Inc., Shutterstock, Spoon Graphics
Cover photographs: iStockphoto, Shutterstock, Spoon Graphics
Interior photographs: Alamy, pp. 9 (left), 19, 25; AP Images, p. 29; iStockphoto, p. 4; Shutterstock, pp. 5 (all), 7, 8 (left, right), 9 (right), 11, 13, 15, 16 (inset), 21, 27; Wikimedia Commons, p. 16

Library of Congress Control Number: 2017961584

Publisher's Cataloging-in-Publication Data
Names: Thomas, Rachael L., author.
Title: Uncovering ancient artifacts / by Rachael L. Thomas.
Description: Minneapolis, Minnesota : Abdo Publishing, 2019. I Series: Excavation
    exploration I Includes online resources and index.
Identifiers: ISBN 9781532115271 (lib.bdg.) I ISBN 9781532155994 (ebook)
Subjects: LCSH: Artifacts (Antiquities--Juvenile literature. I Archaeology--Juvenile
    literature. I Discovery and exploration--Juvenile literature. I Excavations
    (Archaeology)--Juvenile literature.
Classification: DDC 930.10--dc23

CONTENTS

JUNGLE
TREASURE

YOU AND YOUR TEAM HAVE BEEN TRUDGING THROUGH THICK JUNGLE FOR ALMOST A WEEK. The journey has been tough. The path is steep and the ground uneven. Colorful birds chirp from above as you climb.

Thousands of years ago, a king and his subjects ruled these lands. You've poured over maps and ancient writings for many months. You've been trying to find where to search for the remains of this lost nation. Your research brought you here.

Suddenly, you notice a slab of stone emerging from the ground. It is covered with moss and dirt. As you clean the slab, you uncover a line of writing. Your heart leaps. Could this be an ancient artifact? With shovels and brushes, you begin to dig for more.

Your team will help uncover a lost civilization from the objects its people left behind. This discovery is far more than an old rock. It is a window into history!

WHAT ARE
ANCIENT ARTIFACTS?

An artifact is an object that was created by humans long ago. Many artifacts are buried underground. Others were buried but became exposed by wind, rain, and other forces of erosion. Archaeologists search for artifacts on the surface and underground.

An artifact can tell researchers much about the civilization that used it. For example, medicines show which illnesses people suffered. Art shows what was important to a society. Weapons can give clues about how people hunted or fought in wars.

Once artifacts are found, they are often removed and transported to labs or museums. This must be done with great care. Temperature changes, **humidity**, and improper handling can harm artifacts.

It is archaeologists' job to take care of artifacts as they handle them. The amazing items these scientists find are hugely important. They teach us about the world and the people who lived long before us!

Not all artifacts remain intact over time. Those made from harder materials are often what survive. This can include pottery, jewelry, tools, and more.

TIMELINE

1821-1822

Jean-François Champollion publishes his findings from studying the Rosetta Stone text.

1947

A shepherd discovers ancient scrolls in a cave near the Dead Sea. They become known as the Dead Sea Scrolls.

1879

Spanish nobleman Marcelino Sanz de Sautuola discovers wall paintings in the Cave of Altamira.

1974

Emperor Qin Shihuangdi's **Terra-Cotta** Army is discovered in northwestern China.

1990

US law gives Native American tribes rightful ownership of **cultural** artifacts.

2005

The **Terra-Cotta** Army is free of fungus, thanks to **innovations** in artifact conservation.

1982

Archaeologists use a floating crane to lift the *Mary Rose* from the sea south of England.

2011

Scientists report using Google Earth to find thousands of tombs in the Saudi Arabian desert.

CHAPTER 2

ANCIENT ART

Archaeological activity can be traced back to the 1400s and 1500s in Italy. Members of the Italian church began collecting art from ancient Greece and Rome for display. Soon, other European countries began to search for similar artwork. However, these early investigations were done more for the purpose of art collection than for scientific study.

Formal archaeology began with the excavation of Greek and Roman sites in the 1700s. In the following centuries, scientists have uncovered countless pieces of ancient art. Greek pottery has been especially abundant.

Once considered an everyday tool, Greek pottery is now prized by historians. This is because

DIG THIS!

The François Vase is a famous piece of Greek pottery. In 1900, the artifact was smashed into 638 pieces in a protest by a museum guard. Thankfully, it was expertly restored and is still on display in Italy today.

ancient artwork represents the **culture** of the society in which it was made. The styles of Greek pottery artifacts reflect popular trends in ancient Greece. The scenes, **inscriptions**, and other details on the objects also provide visual information. They can give clues about popular food, clothing, and activities of the time.

Clay pots were everyday objects in ancient Greece. They were used for practical purposes, such as storing water and wine.

Greek pottery is generally dated between 2,000 and 3,000 years old. But humans have been creating artwork for much longer. In 1879, older artwork was discovered in a cave in northern Spain.

This cave is called the Cave of Altamira. It was first excavated by Spanish nobleman Marcelino Sanz de Sautuola. He uncovered stone tools and animal bones from the cave floor.

Later, Sanz de Sautuola visited the cave with his daughter. She noticed drawings on its walls. The drawings showed animals such as horses and bison. Sanz de Sautuola believed the cave paintings were important artifacts. He published his findings in 1880.

Archaeologists thought the cave paintings looked too modern compared to other ancient cave paintings. But in 1902, experts concluded that the paintings were prehistoric. Before this discovery, prehistoric humans were thought to be more like animals than modern humans. The cave paintings proved this idea wrong. They showed that early humans were intelligent and artistic.

Excavations of the cave continued through the 1900s. More recently, scientists have dated the **charcoal** in the black paint used for the paintings. They estimate the paintings are about 14,000 years old!

The National Museum and Research Center of Altamira displays a reproduction of the Cave of Altamira. Visitors can view copies of the paintings in a life-size cave exhibit.

CHAPTER 3

ANCIENT WRITINGS

By the 1900s, archaeology had become a worldwide study. Artifacts were no longer seen simply as valuable items for sale and display. Scientists now understood that artifacts were key pieces of human history that needed protection.

One of these artifacts was uncovered in 1947. That year, a shepherd discovered a cave near the Dead Sea between Israel and Jordan. Inside the cave he found jars containing ancient scrolls.

Further exploration uncovered the remains of more than 900 scrolls in surrounding caves. They became known as the Dead Sea Scrolls. These artifacts were made of plant fibers and animal skins. They had been preserved in the caves for around 2,000 years!

DIG THIS!

Early researchers used tape to connect various pieces of the Dead Sea Scrolls. Over time, the tape caused further damage to the delicate scrolls. Scientists today are still working to remove the tape and better preserve the scrolls.

The Dead Sea Scrolls provide detailed information about ancient life in the Middle East. They also include the earliest known pieces of writing from the Hebrew bible. The scrolls have helped historians understand the origins of Judaism, Christianity, and Islam.

Some of the Dead Sea Scrolls are now housed in the Israel Museum in Jerusalem. They are located in a wing of the museum called Shrine of the Book.

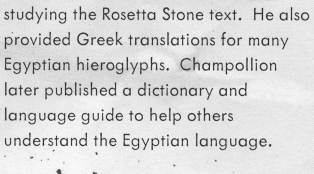

JEAN-FRANÇOIS CHAMPOLLION

Jean-François Champollion was born in France in 1790. By 16 years old, he had mastered Latin, Greek, and six other ancient languages. He later used his knowledge of language to translate the Egyptian script found on the Rosetta Stone.

From 1821 to 1822, Champollion published his findings from studying the Rosetta Stone text. He also provided Greek translations for many Egyptian hieroglyphs. Champollion later published a dictionary and language guide to help others understand the Egyptian language.

Ancient writings can also be keys to lost languages. In ancient Egypt, people wrote using pictures and symbols called hieroglyphs. But for centuries, scholars could not understand the meaning of Egyptian hieroglyphs. It was a lost language.

The discovery of the Rosetta Stone in 1799 solved this problem. A Frenchman found the stone near the town of Rosetta in Egypt. The black slab was **inscribed** with both Egyptian and Greek text.

Language expert Jean-François Champollion studied the artifact. He used his knowledge of the Greek language to translate the Egyptian hieroglyphs. This was a major advancement for historians. A lost language now had meaning. And like the Dead Sea Scrolls, the Rosetta Stone shed new light on an ancient **culture**.

UNDERWATER
ARTIFACTS

As archaeology tools and **technologies** advanced, researchers excavated more challenging sites. Underwater sites required special tools and skills to safely recover artifacts. Some of these methods were used during the 1970s excavation of the *Mary Rose*.

The *Mary Rose* was an English ship from the 1500s. It sank during a battle with the French in 1545. Divers discovered the ship off the southern coast of England in 1971.

The entire shipwreck was removed from the sea in 1982. The *Mary Rose* and its contents were soaked with water. So, scientists used a special spray that replaced water in the wood with wax. Some items were also **freeze-dried**.

DIG THIS!

Artifacts found in the *Mary Rose* provided a window into life in England in the 1500s. Researchers uncovered board games, musical instruments, and other possessions. The skeleton of a dog was also found among the wreckage.

These methods helped advance common practices in marine excavation. They also furthered knowledge of how to preserve waterlogged artifacts. From discovery to display, the *Mary Rose* project was an important step in modern marine archaeology.

Archaeologists used a floating crane to carefully lift the *Mary Rose* from the sea. Then, a barge carried the ship to shore.

CHAPTER 5

BURIAL SITES

Some artifacts are found in accidental graves, such as sunken ships. Others are buried in purposeful graves. In some **cultures**, it was a sign of respect to bury a person with valuable objects. For others, it was thought that items buried with the dead would be taken into the afterlife.

One of the most famous burial sites today was built for Qin Shihuangdi, the first emperor of China. Qin died in 210 BCE. But before his death, he wished for an entire army to accompany him to the afterlife! Now named the **Terra-Cotta** Army, about 8,000 clay soldiers were stationed near Qin's tomb. The army also included horses, **chariots**, and acrobats.

The Terra-Cotta Army was discovered in northwestern China in 1974. It was one of the most exciting artifact discoveries of recent times. Archaeologists across the world were amazed by the size of Qin's burial grounds. Researchers removed 3,510,000 cubic feet (99,000 cu m) of earth when excavating the site!

The terra-cotta soldiers display a wide range of facial features and hairstyles. Experts believe the figures may have been based on members of a real army.

The discovery provided historians with valuable information about life in ancient China. The soldiers were buried with about 40,000 bronze weapons. These weapons taught researchers about ancient Chinese metalwork and resources. The formation of the soldiers displayed ancient Chinese battle tactics.

Archaeologists located Qin's tomb using ground-penetrating radar. The tomb is separate from the chambers that held the **Terra-Cotta** Army. But the Chinese emperor has been left untouched by excavators.

Archaeologists have learned that excavating a site can damage the artifacts preserved within it. So, researchers today are less likely to excavate sites when it is not considered necessary or appropriate. Some argue that Qin's tomb should be opened once excavation tools are more advanced. Others believe the tomb should never be opened and the emperor should be left in peace.

THE EMPEROR'S TOMB COMPLEX

Ground-penetrating radar revealed Qin's tomb complex to be nearly 38 square miles (98 sq km). The **Terra-Cotta** Army lies almost 1 mile (1.6 km) outside the outer wall of the complex.

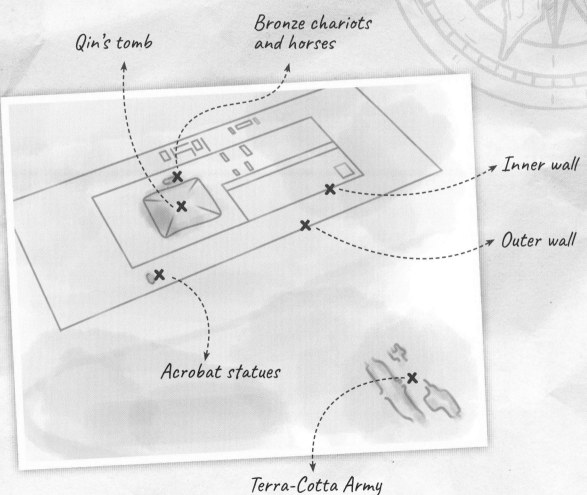

Qin's tomb

Bronze chariots and horses

Inner wall

Outer wall

Acrobat statues

Terra-Cotta Army

TOOLS & TECH

Archaeologists have learned to explore ancient sites without damaging them. Advanced tools and **technologies** have made this easier. One of these tools is ground-penetrating radar.

Ground-penetrating radar uses radio waves to locate underground objects. An artifact buried in the ground will reflect the radio waves. This method allows researchers to locate artifacts without digging and possibly damaging the objects.

Archaeologists use **X-ray** technology to discover what an artifact is made of. The artifact absorbs energy from the X-rays. The object then gives off new X-rays. These rays differ depending on what material the artifact is made of. This method is useful when an artifact's origin is unknown. Knowing an artifact's chemical makeup can help lead archaeologists to where it came from.

Some archaeological devices are available for everybody to use. One such device is Google Earth. This **satellite** system allows users to view remote regions of Earth. Archaeologists can now

Ground-penetrating radar measures the time it takes radar pulses to reflect off of underground objects. This tells scientists how deep underground artifacts are.

locate ancient sites without physically searching the area. In 2011, scientists reported using Google Earth to find thousands of tombs in the Saudi Arabian desert!

Scientific advances have also allowed for new methods of conserving artifacts. One of these methods helps restore artifacts damaged by fungus. Fungus grows when artifacts are exposed to changes in temperature and **humidity**. Over time, certain fungi produce acids that can damage artifacts.

Twenty years ago, fungus was damaging the statues of the **Terra-Cotta** Army. In 1999, scientists at a Belgium lab began working on a solution to this problem. They had been developing anti-fungal **formulas** for fruits, vegetables, and other crops. Now, they altered their formulas so they could safely remove fungus from ancient artifacts.

Researchers sprayed the anti-fungal formula into the soils around the clay soldiers. By 2005, the Terra-Cotta Army was free of fungus. **Innovations** like these ensure that precious artifacts can be studied for many years to come.

The terra-cotta soldiers are displayed in a museum built around the discovery site. But, researchers worry that air pollutants and heat are interfering with the preservation of the artifacts.

CLAIMING
HISTORY

Advances in archaeology have allowed the excavation and conservation of all kinds of artifacts. However, the removal and study of artifacts can create problems. One issue concerns ownership of artifacts.

Many archaeologists excavate sites in regions where they do not live. Artifacts found in these sites may then be sold to museums and universities in other countries. Communities around the world have fought to have artifacts returned to where they came from.

Many countries have passed laws relating to artifact ownership. One was created in 1990. It is called the Native American Graves Protection and **Repatriation** Act (NAGPRA).

When Europeans first settled in the United States, they stole land and possessions from Native Americans. Burial grounds were **disturbed** and artifacts removed. According to NAGPRA, Native American tribes can now claim these artifacts. Thousands of items have been returned to tribes because of NAGPRA.

In 2016, the United States returned more than 200 artifacts to India. A ceremony in Washington, DC, marked the occasion.

Ownership continues to be an important issue in artifact discovery and study. Since 2007, the United States has returned more than 8,000 artifacts to their rightful home countries. These actions are important victories for archaeology. Each physical piece of the past reveals more of a nation's, and the world's, history.

GLOSSARY

charcoal — a black material that is a form of carbon.

chariot — a two-wheeled horse-drawn carriage commonly used in ancient battles.

culture — the customs, arts, and tools of a nation or a people at a certain time. Something related to culture is cultural.

disturb — to interfere with or interrupt.

formula — a combination of specific amounts of different ingredients or elements.

freeze-dry — to remove water from an object by freezing it in a vacuum. The water then turns from ice to vapor.

humidity — the amount of moisture in the air.

innovation — a new idea, method, or device.

inscription — something written or engraved on a surface. To make an inscription is to inscribe.

repatriation — the return to a country or place of origin.

satellite — a manufactured object that orbits Earth. A satellite relays scientific information back to Earth.

technology (tehk-NAH-luh-jee) — a machine or piece of equipment created using science and engineering, and made to do certain tasks.

terra-cotta — a baked clay used for pottery, statues, and building materials.

X-ray — an invisible and powerful light wave that can pass through solid objects.

ONLINE RESOURCES

Booklinks
NONFICTION
NETWORK
FREE! ONLINE NONFICTION RESOURCES

To learn more about ancient artifacts, visit **abdobooklinks.com**. These links are routinely monitored and updated to provide the most current information available.

INDEX